WILDLIFE IN BLOOM SERIES

Little Bat

BY AUTHOR & CONSERVATIONIST

LINDA BLACKMOOR

© 2024 BY LINDA BLACKMOOR

ALL RIGHTS RESERVED. NO PORTION OF THIS BOOK MAY BE REPRODUCED, STORED IN RETRIEVAL SYSTEM, OR TRANSMITTED IN ANY FORM OR BY ANY MEANS - ELECTRONIC, MECHANICAL, PHOTOCOPY, RECORDING, SCANNING, OR OTHER - EXCEPT FOR BRIEF QUESTIONS IN CRITICAL REVIEWS OR ARTICLES, WITHOUT THE PRIOR WRITTEN PERMISSION OF THE PUBLISHER OR AUTHOR.

ISBN: 978-1-966417-07-1 (PRINT)

PUBLISHED BY QUILL PRESS. LINDA BLACKMOOR'S TITLES MAY BE PURCHASED IN BULK FOR EDUCATIONAL, BUSINESS, FUNDRAISING, OR SALES PROMOTIONAL USE. FOR INFORMATION, PLEASE EMAIL HELLO@LINDABLACKMOOR.COM

FIRST PRINT EDITION: 2024

LINDA BLACKMOOR
WWW.LINDABLACKMOOR.COM

BAT FACTS #1

SPECIES

Bats are mammals of the order Chiroptera, meaning "hand-wing" in Greek, encompassing over 1,400 species worldwide. They are the second-largest order of mammals after rodents, representing about 20% of all mammal species. Bats inhabit every continent except Antarctica, thriving in habitats from deserts to tropical rainforests They include insectivores, frugivores, nectar-feeders, and even carnivores.

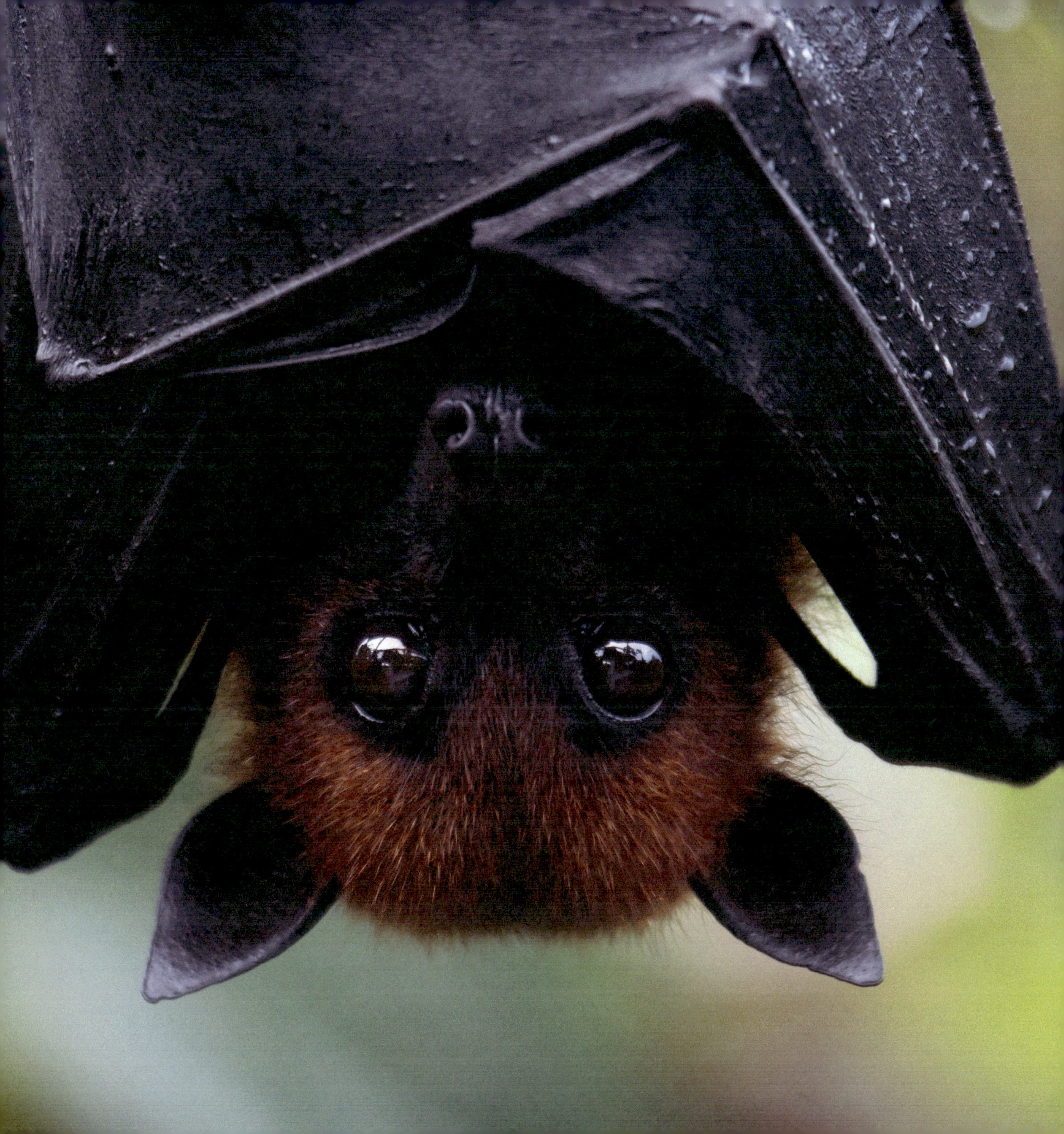

BAT FACTS #2
ECHOES

Many bats use echolocation, emitting high-frequency sounds that bounce off objects, allowing them to navigate and hunt in complete darkness. Their specialized ears detect the returning echoes, helping them determine the size, shape, and distance of obstacles and prey. Echolocation pulses can reach frequencies up to 120 kilohertz, far beyond human hearing. This ability enables them to catch insects mid-flight.

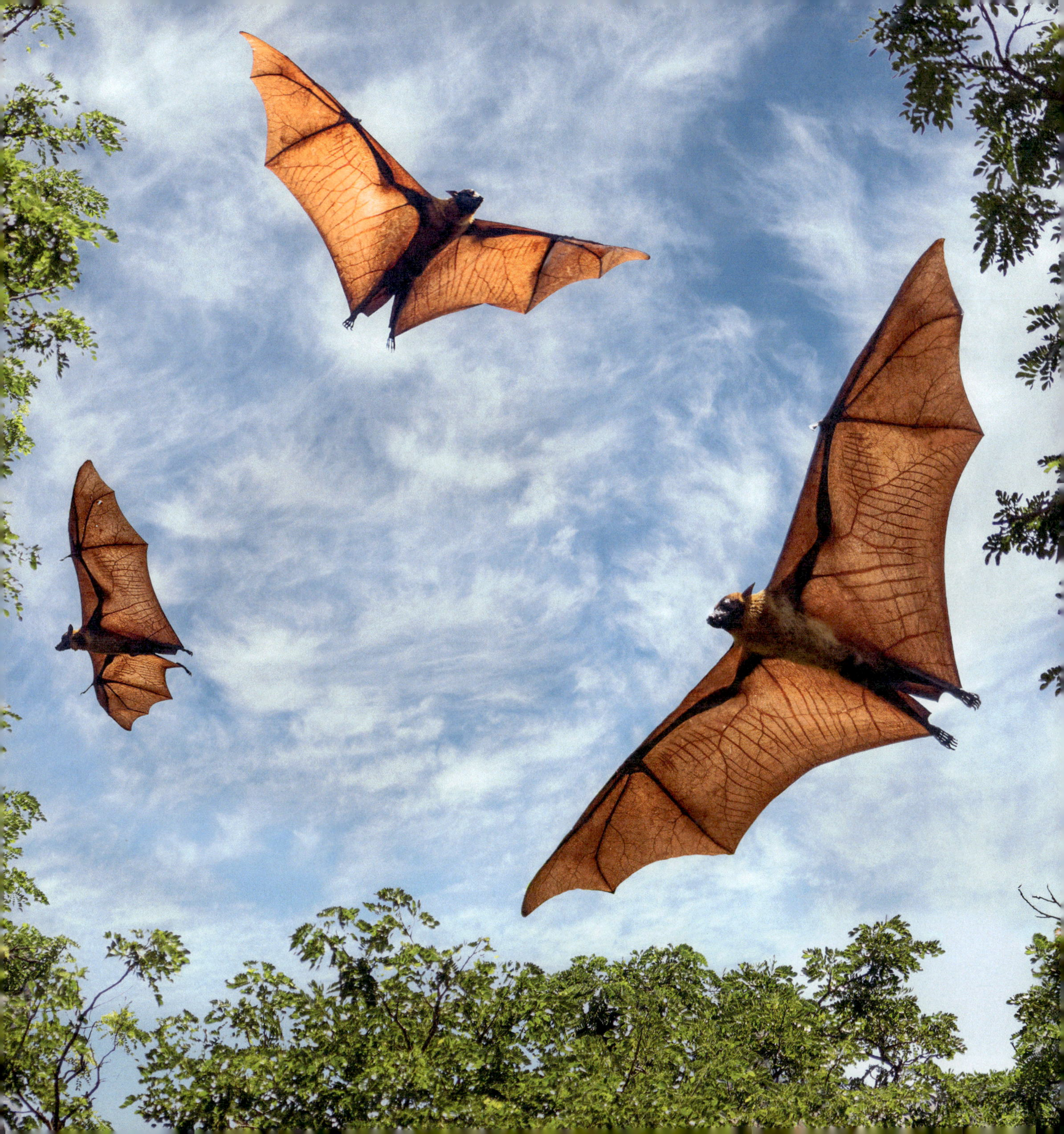

BAT FACTS #3

FLIGHT

Bats are the only mammals capable of sustained flight, with wings formed by stretched skin over elongated finger bones. Their wings are highly flexible, allowing precise maneuvering and agility unmatched by most birds. Bats can fly at speeds up to 60 miles per hour and even hover or fly backward. Their unique wing structure also aids in thermoregulation by allowing heat exchange through the thin membrane.

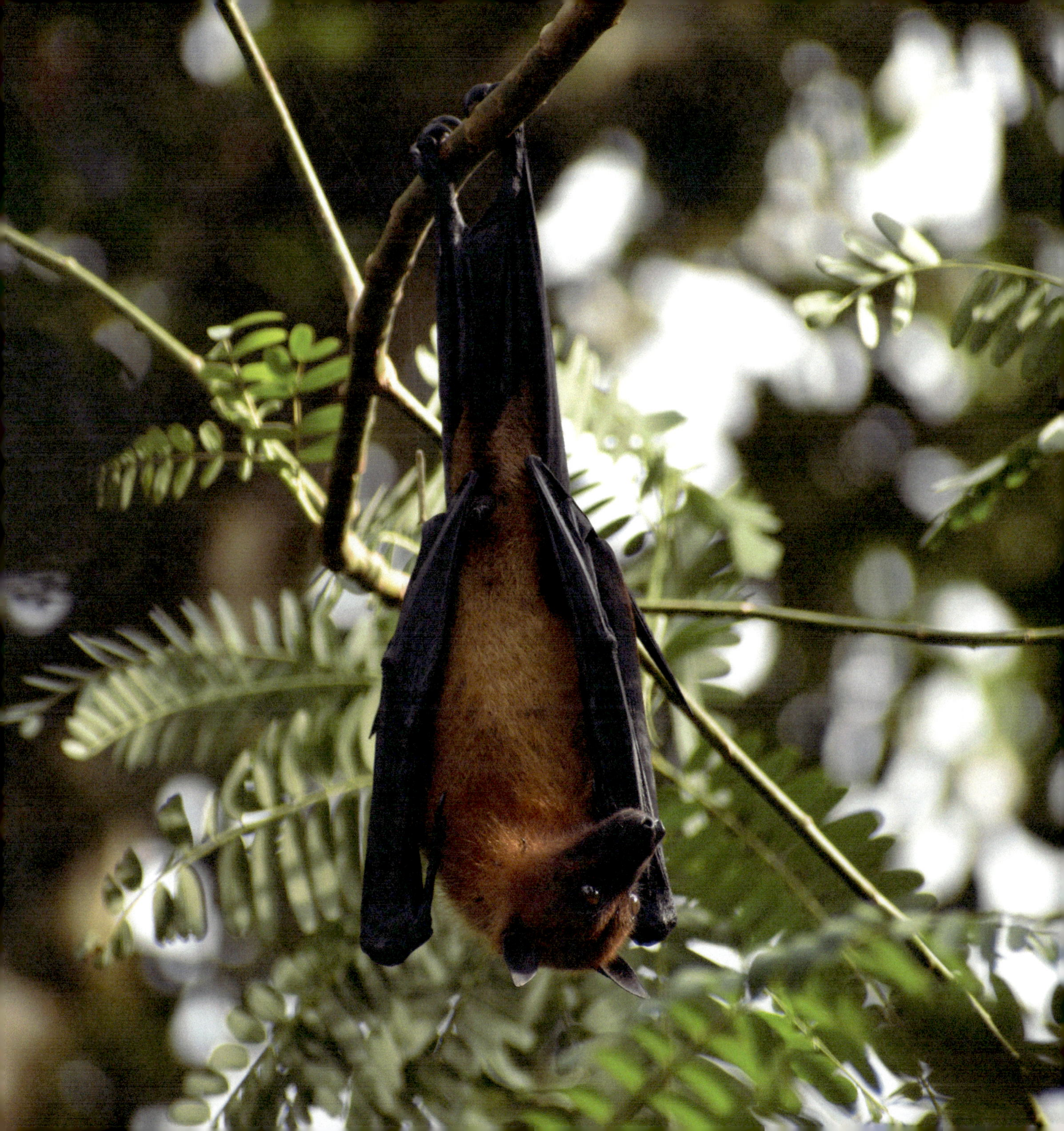

BAT FACTS #4

DIET

Bats have diverse diets, with species feeding on insects, fruit, nectar, pollen, fish, and even other small animals. Insect-eating bats can consume up to 1,000 mosquitoes in a single hour, significantly helping control pest populations. Fruit bats, also known as flying foxes, play vital roles in seed dispersal and forest regeneration. Some species, like the greater bulldog bat, have adapted to catch fish.

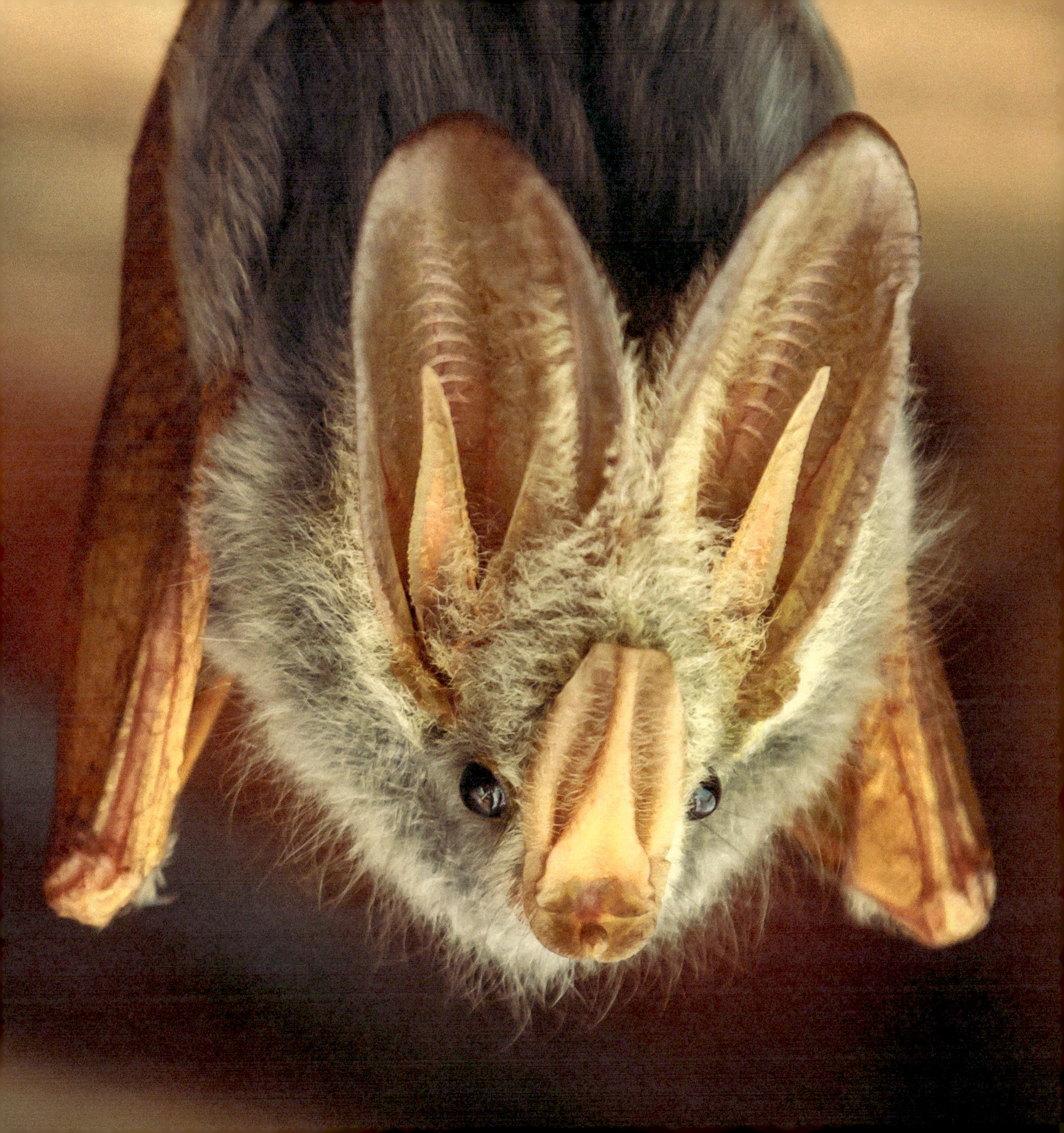

BAT FACTS #5

POLLINATE

Some bats are essential pollinators, aiding over 500 plant species including bananas, mangoes, and agave used for making tequila. They have long snouts and tongues adapted to reach deep into flowers, collecting and transferring pollen as they feed on nectar. Bat-pollinated flowers often bloom at night and emit strong scents to attract them.

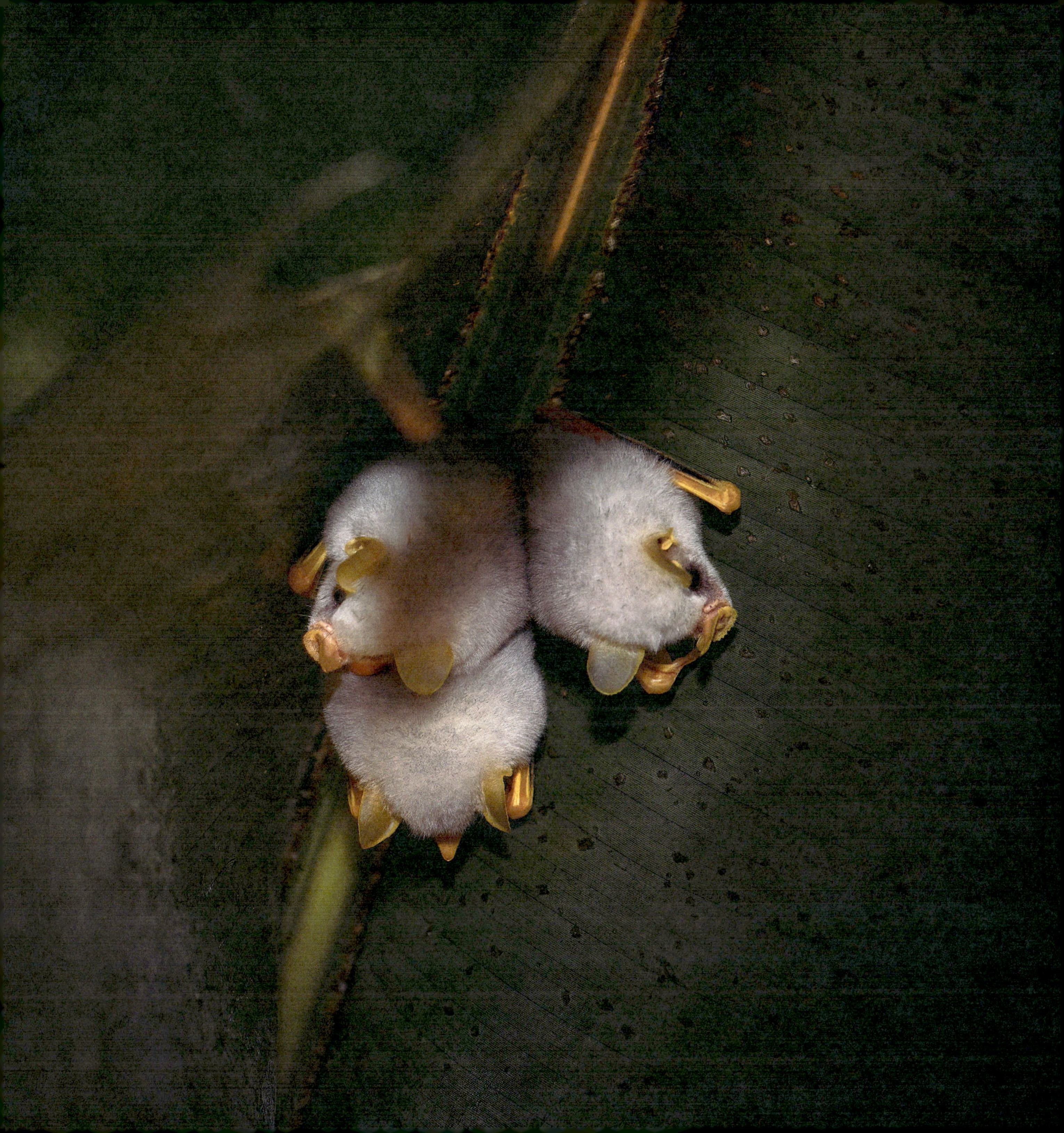

BAT FACTS #6
ROOST

Bats roost in various places like caves, tree hollows, under bridges, and even in buildings, often hanging upside down. Hanging allows them to take flight quickly by simply dropping into the air, essential since their hind limbs are not well-suited for takeoff from the ground. Roosting sites provide safety from predators and harsh weather, and some species form colonies of millions of individuals.

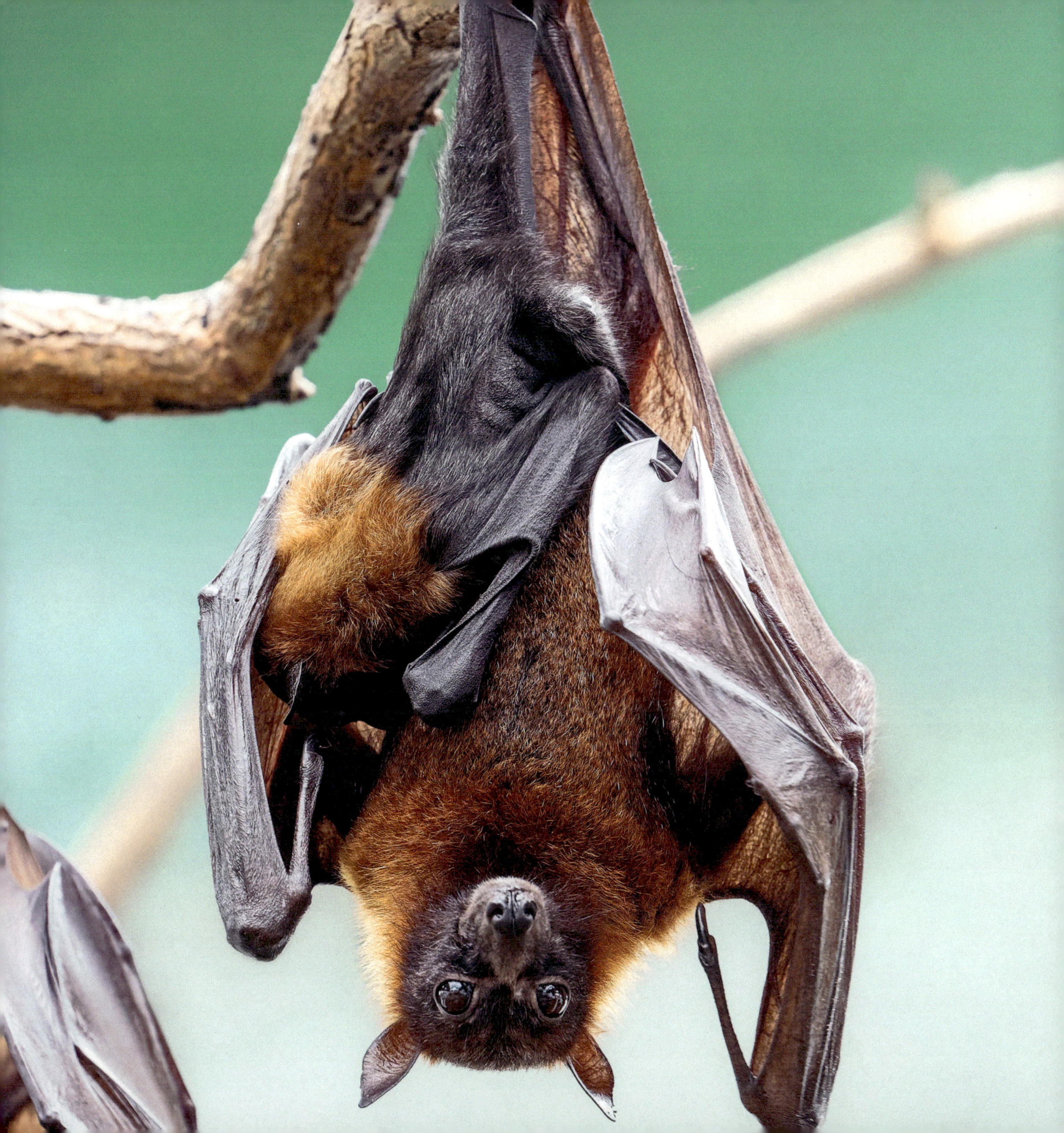

BAT FACTS #7

SENSES

Besides echolocation, bats have keen senses of smell and hearing, with some species also possessing good eyesight. Fruit bats rely more on vision and smell to locate food, as they do not use echolocation. Their large ears and specialized nose structures enhance sound reception for navigation and hunting. Some species can even detect ultraviolet light, aiding in locating flowers and ripe fruit.

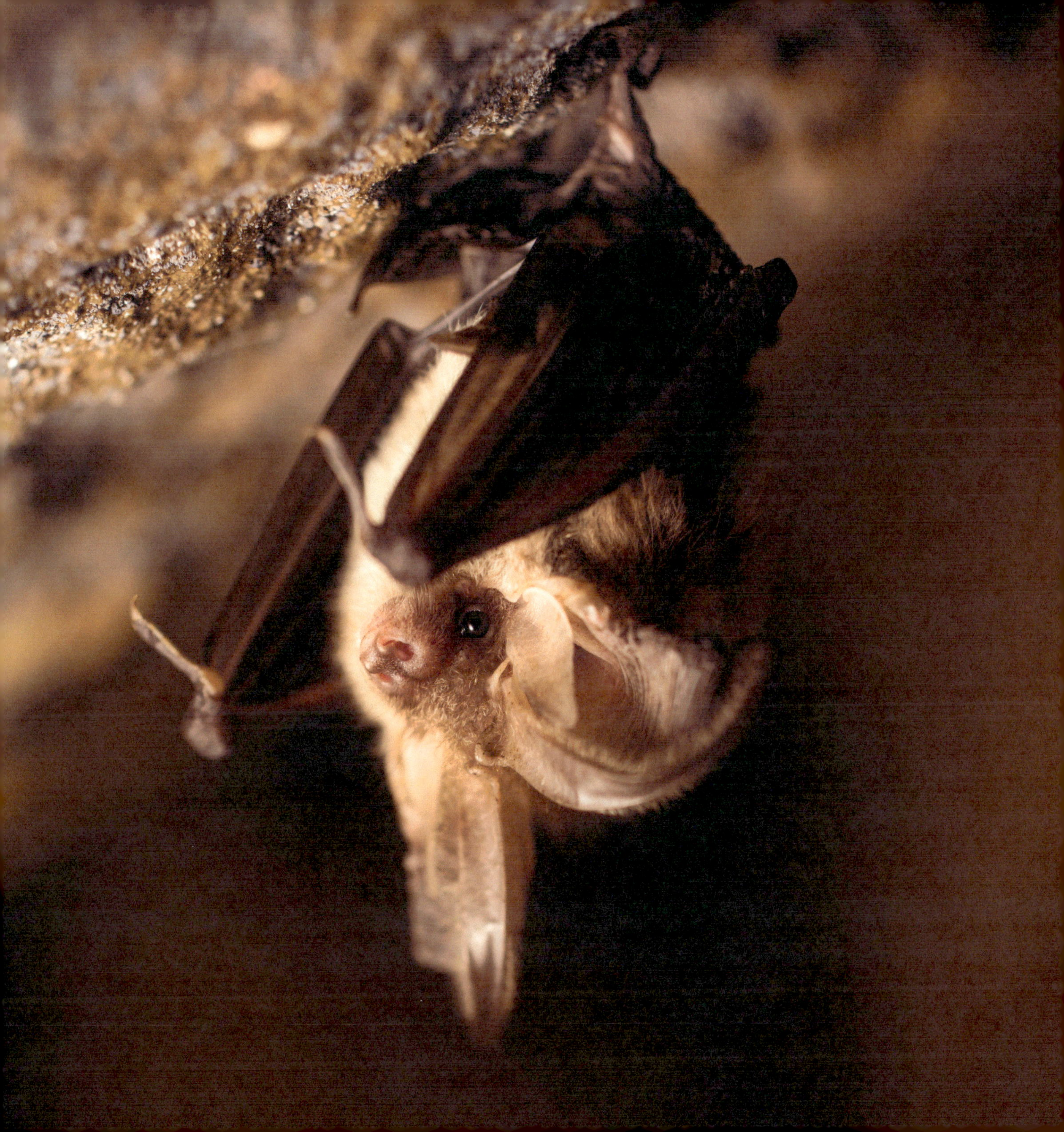

BAT FACTS #8
LIFESPAN

Bats have surprisingly long lifespans for their size, with some species living over 30 years in the wild. The Brandt's bat holds the record for longevity, reaching up to 41 years despite weighing less than a penny. Their slow metabolism and ability to hibernate contribute to their extended lifespans. Longevity studies in bats help scientists understand aging processes in mammals.

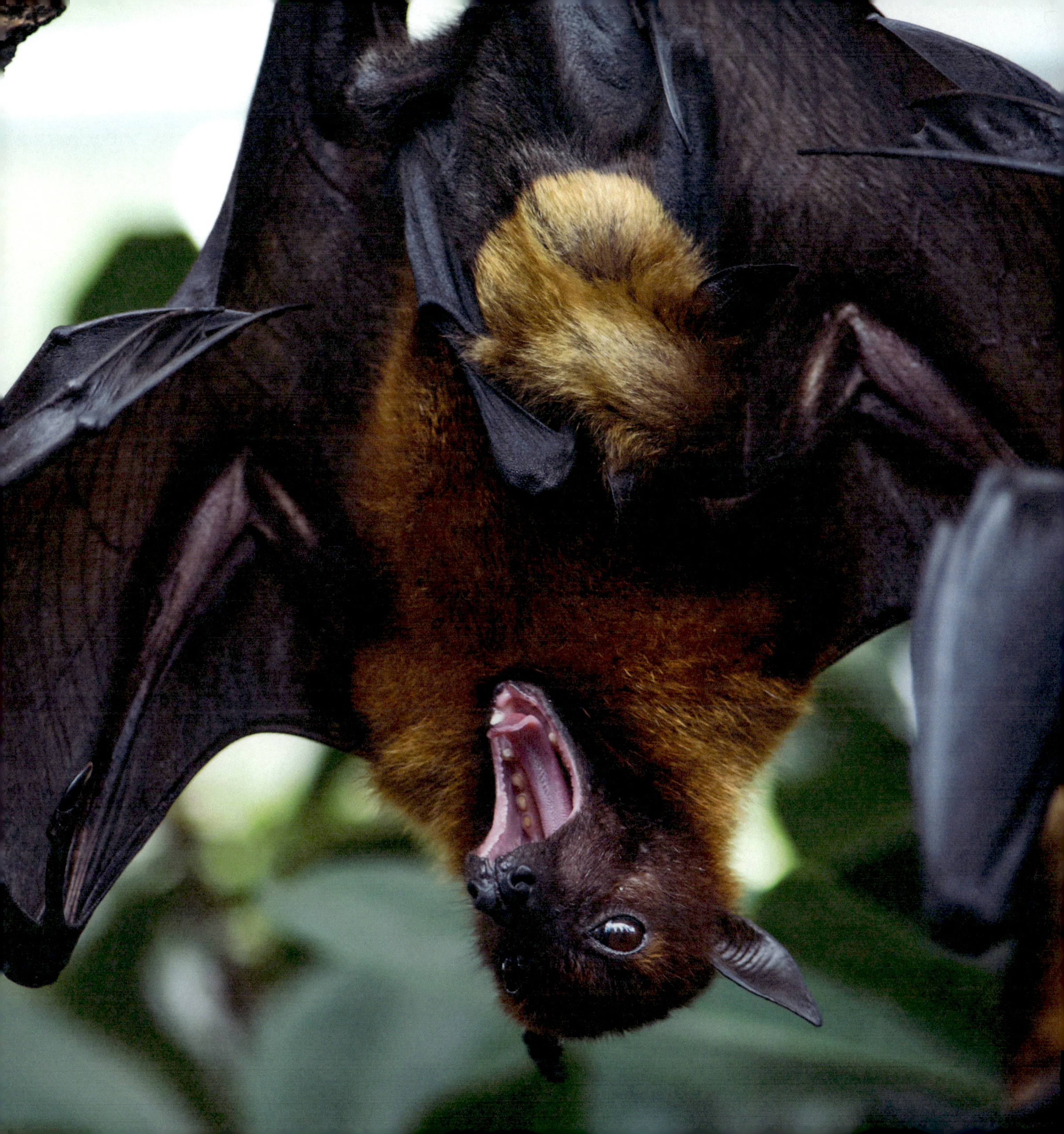

BAT FACTS #9

SIZE

Bats vary greatly in size, from the tiny bumblebee bat weighing less than 2 grams to the giant flying foxes with wingspans up to 6 feet. The bumblebee bat, found in Thailand and Myanmar, is the world's smallest mammal by weight. Flying foxes, native to tropical regions, are among the largest bats but feed exclusively on fruit and nectar. Size variations among bat species are adaptations to their ecology.

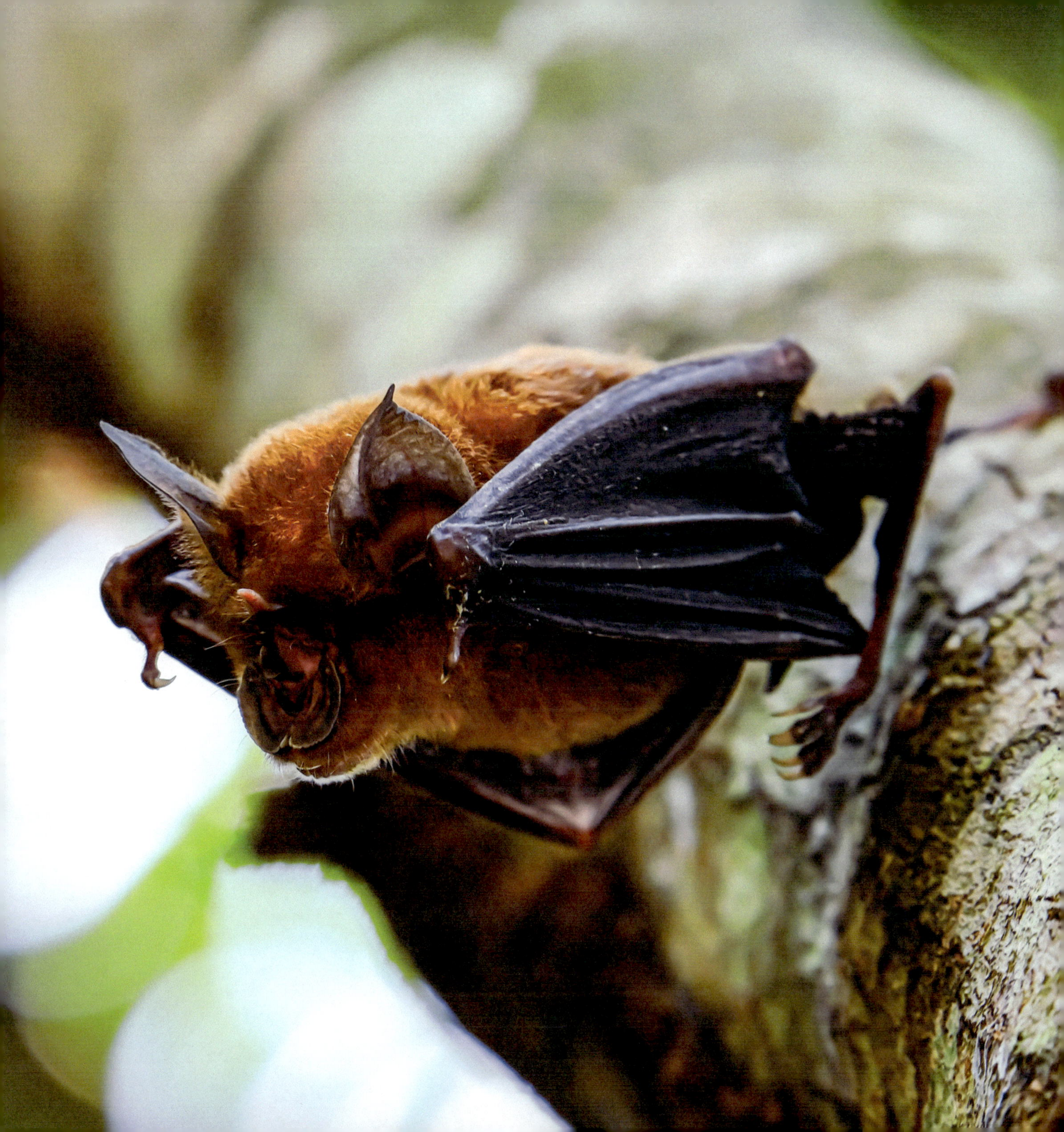

BAT FACTS #10
HIBERNATE

Many bats hibernate during cold months, slowing their metabolism and lowering body temperature to conserve energy. They can reduce their heart rate from 400 beats per minute to as few as 10 beats per minute during this state. Hibernation sites must be humid and maintain stable temperatures to prevent dehydration and freezing. During hibernation, some bats may lose half their body weight.

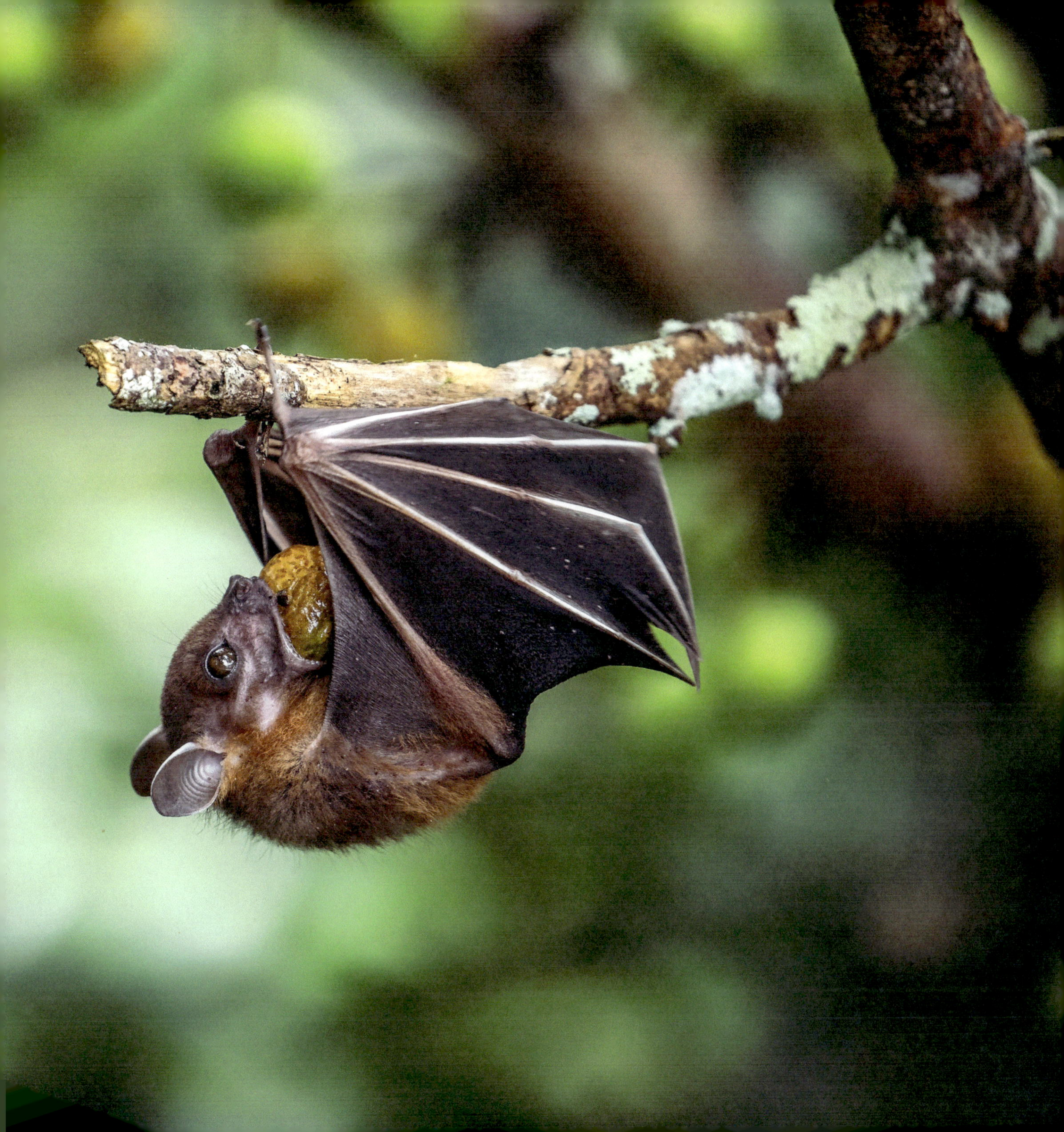

BAT FACTS #11

SOCIAL

Bats exhibit complex social behaviors, forming colonies that can range from a few individuals to millions. They communicate using a variety of vocalizations and even physical contact, grooming each other to strengthen social bonds. Some species display altruistic behavior, such as sharing food with colony members that are unable to feed themselves. The structure in bat colonies can include hierarchical systems.

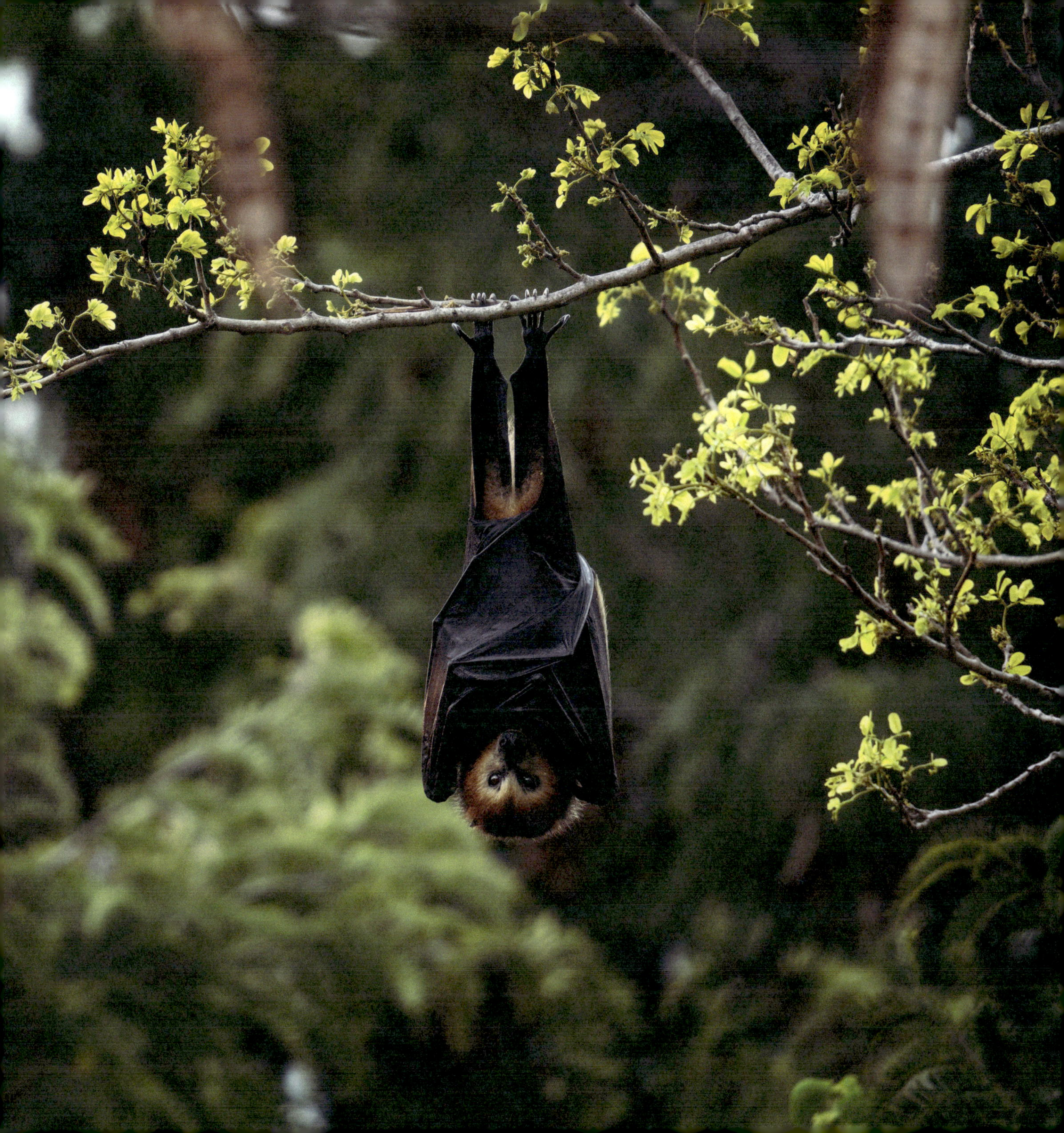

BAT FACTS #12
VAMPIRE

Vampire bats are the only mammals that feed exclusively on blood, using heat sensors and sharp teeth to locate and access blood from their prey. Found in Central and South America, they typically feed on livestock like cows and horses, usually without the host noticing. Their saliva contains anticoagulants called draculin that prevent blood from clotting. Vampire bats can transmit diseases like rabies.

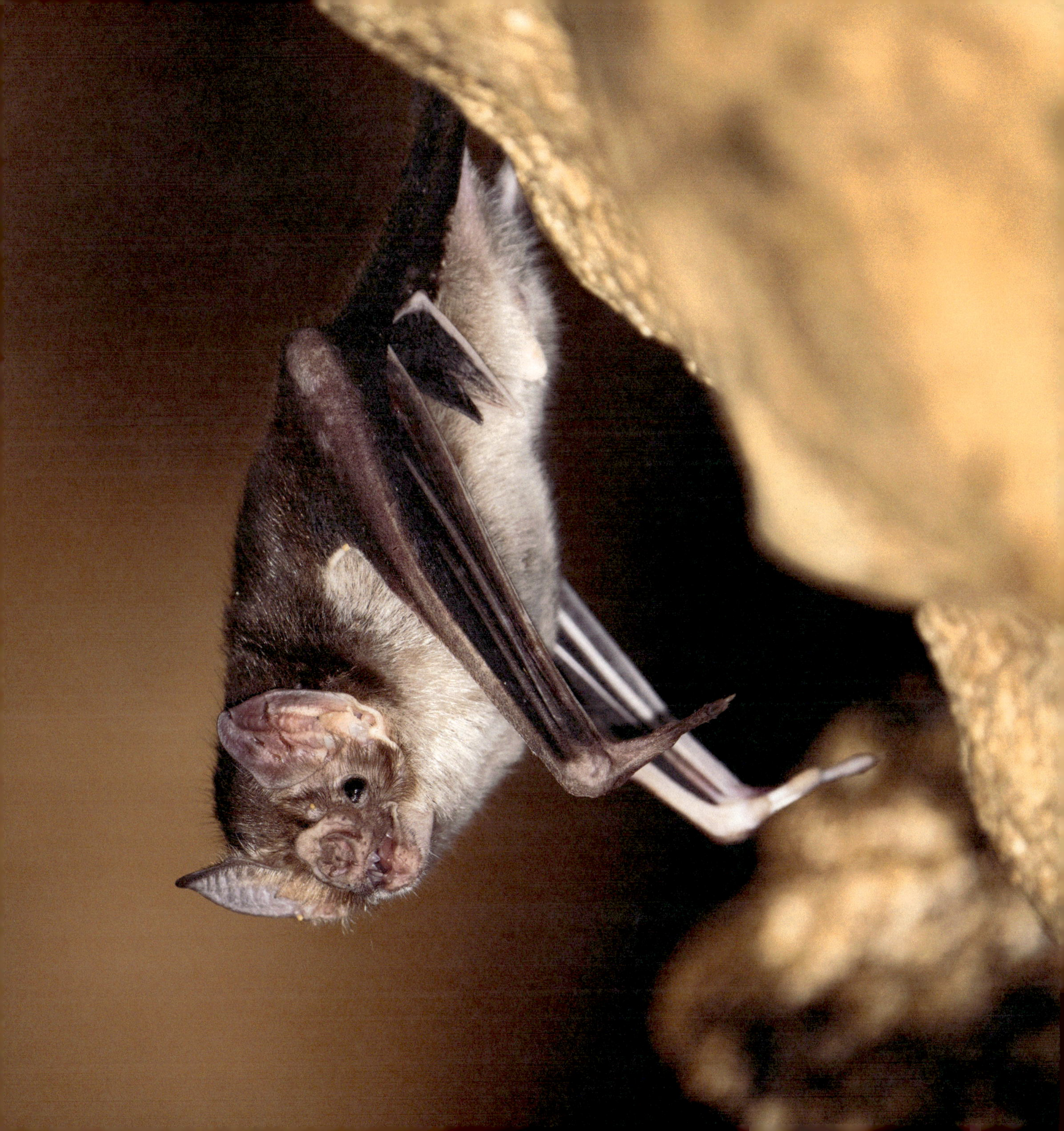

BAT FACTS #13

IMMUNITY

Bats possess an immune system that allows them to carry viruses without becoming ill. Their bodies can host viruses like rabies, Ebola, and coronaviruses while showing no symptoms of disease. Researchers study bats' immune responses to understand how they suppress inflammation and fight infections effectively. This unique immunity helps bats survive in diverse environments.

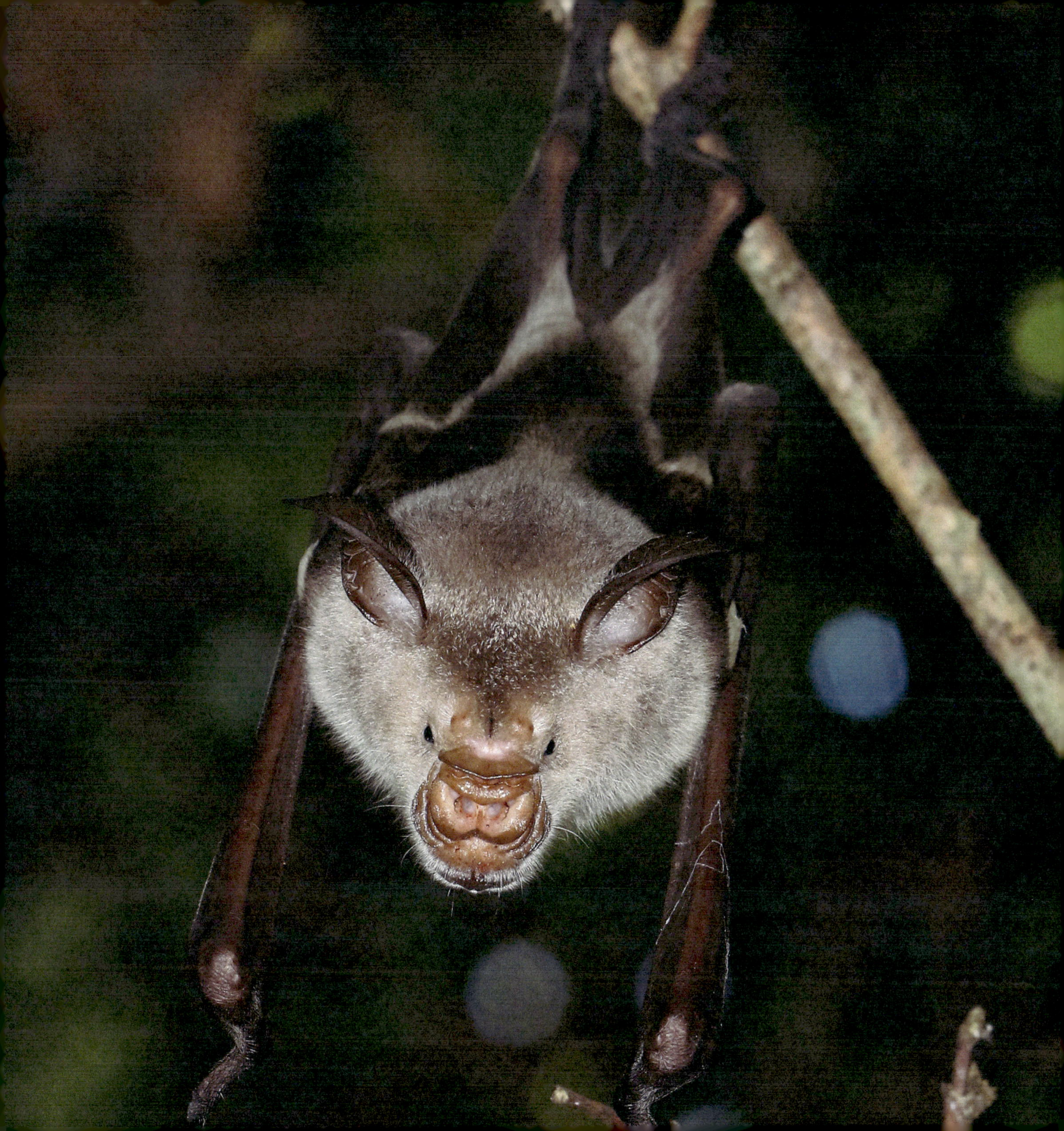

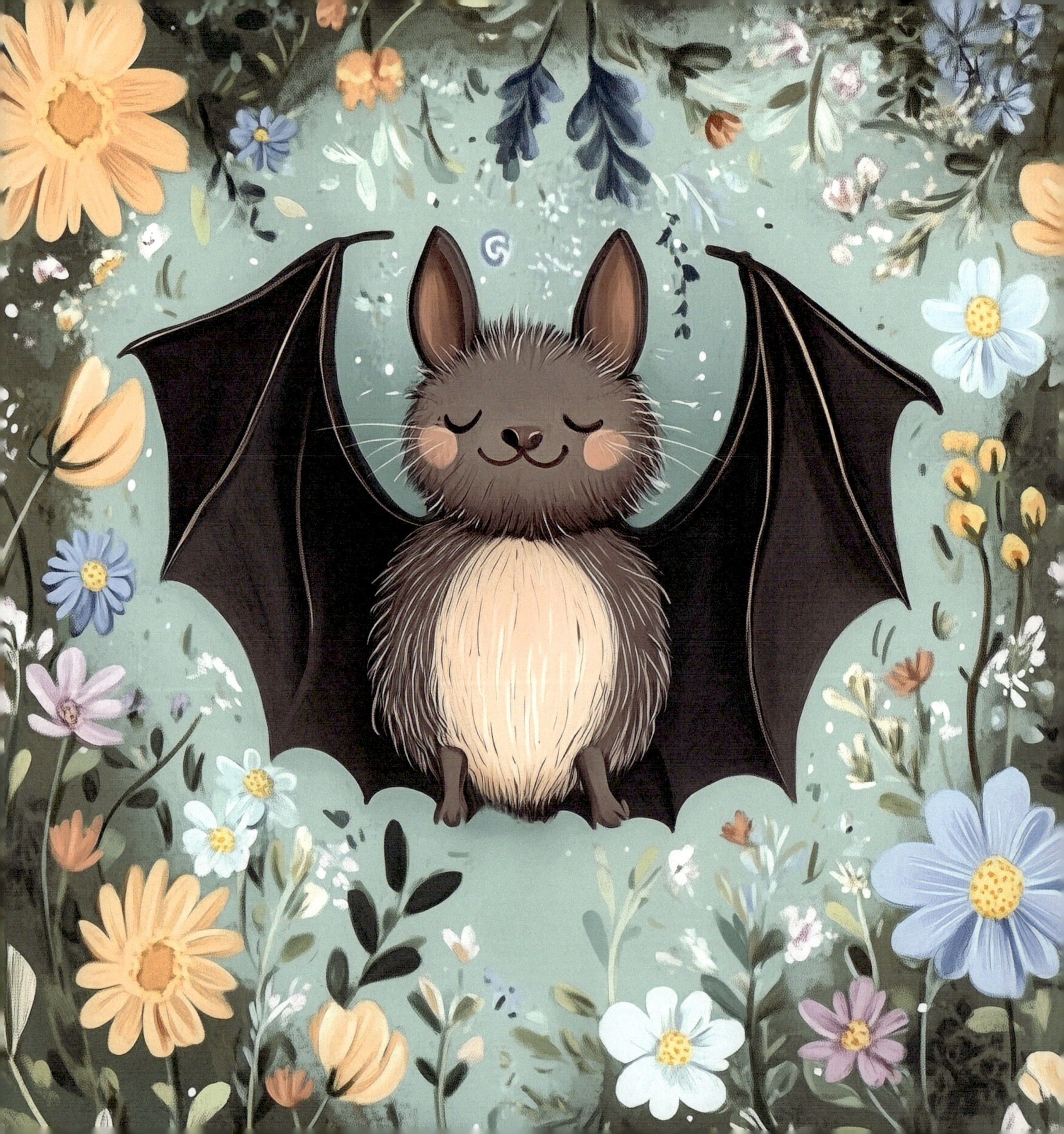

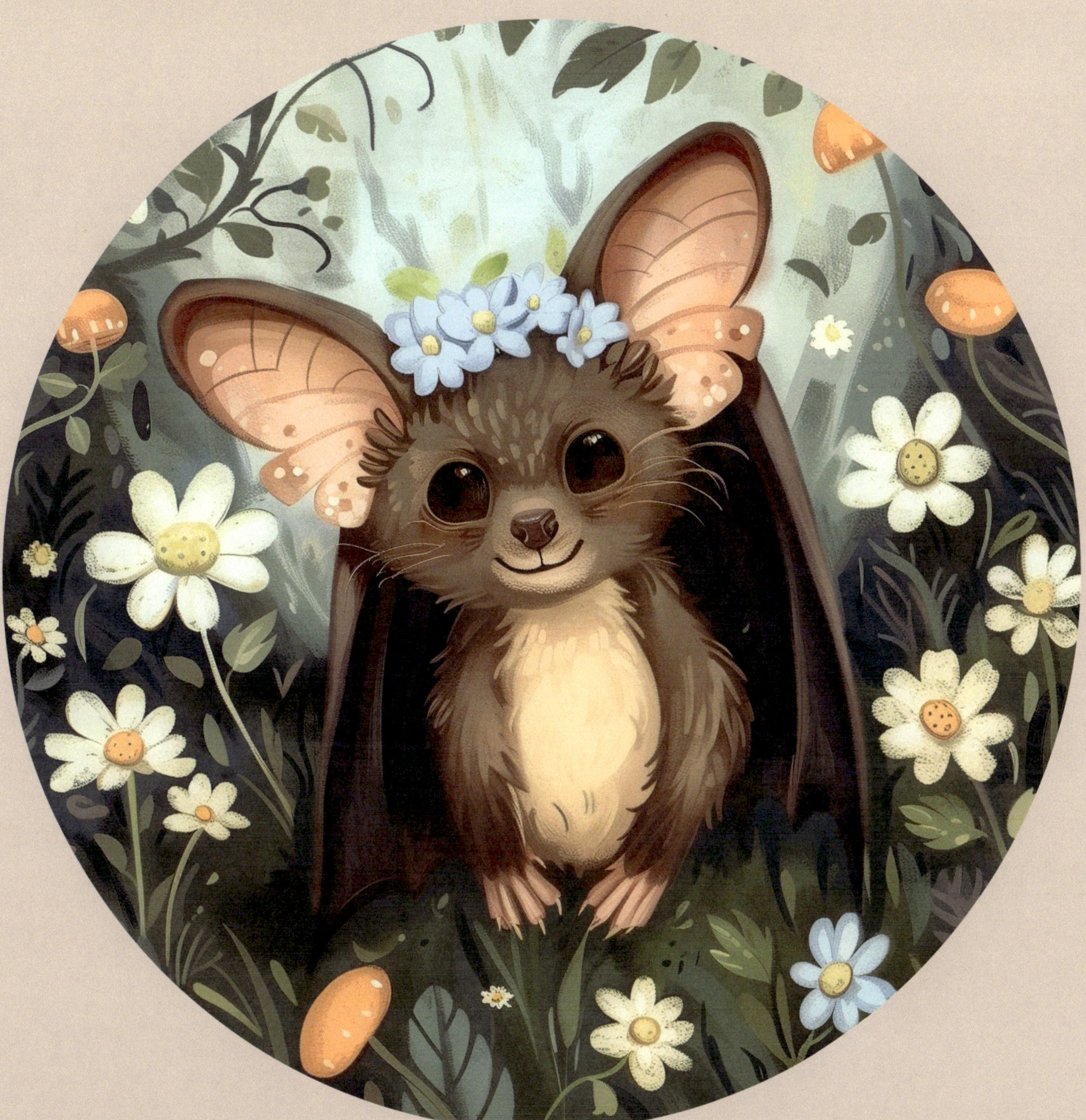

Made in the USA
Columbia, SC
02 May 2025